"Bullet Beans to Big Dreams"

An inspiring story from the girl "off the estate"

Gemma Worth

Published by New Generation Publishing in 2021

First Edition

ISBN

	Paperback	978-1-80031-139-8
	Ebook	978-1-80031-138-1

www.newgeneration-publishing.com

New Generation Publishing

Contents

Credits

Barbara Fulton
Adam Buckley
Kirsty Platts
Alysha Bradley
Ben Riley
Dry Wave Recovery

Dedications

My Dad, the first man I ever loved and the reason I am a strong independent woman.

Dad .... "I'll tell you all about it when I see you again".

Ryan, my little brother, a bond between siblings is stronger than anything, no matter the distance or the years that pass by.

To my forever friend Kirsty, where would I be without you? Eleven years of true friendship and many more years to come. We have endured more in these eleven years than I can remember. We have loved and lost, grieved and gained.

The most special thing of all is you gave me my Godson who I truly adore.

Rhianna, my daughter, my angel in disguise. I would be so lost without you.

Marie and Ian "AKA" Mother and Father, thank you for taking me under your wing.

Ben SOS Riley, I will always be your celebrity wife, love you man.

Author's words

Hello, Gemma here, I want to thank you for taking the time to read my book.

At only thirty-seven you may ask yourself …. Really? Are you not too young to write a book about your life? But honestly, it has been one hell of a ride. ……. I am just a normal girl from a council estate up north, who with hard work, blood, sweat and many tears, has made all her dreams come true.

I decided to embark on my first book because I wanted to inspire likeminded men and women to follow their dreams no matter where they come from, their upbringing or life decisions, and say "you can turn this around". It all starts with a dream, sprinkled with ambition, sheer determination and pure northern grit.

It is sometimes hard to ever see a light at the end of a tunnel but, in life I believe that everything that happens to you is for a reason and it places you on the path you are supposed to be on.

Now, no one said that path would be easy but, the universe works in mysterious ways.

The title of the book you might say is somewhat strange but to me it perfectly describes my childhood, my life.

When I decided to write this book, I began to think of a suitable title then one day whilst thinking of my childhood and Ryan, my Brother, it just came to me. "Bullet Beans" as my brother and I christened our baked beans to which these played a big part of our lives.

As a child of the nineties a big supermarket chain began to sell their own cheaper brand of food. Included in this food brand were baked beans for the price of nine pence a tin. When we were growing up money was tight, and these beans with a slice or two of toast became part of our staple diet, beans on toast.

My brother and I soon nicknamed them bullet beans as they were hard like bullets and to be perfectly honest with you, not at all nice. We had many a food fight with these beans, flicking them across the table at one another. I have very fond memories of my time growing up with Ryan and could not think of a more fitting accolade to our childhood for the title of my book, from how it all began with baked bean food fights to now, me living my dream.

This short story is a raw and personal account of me and my life. I have worked hard for everything I have today and I hope this book gives you an insight of the struggles and traumas I have overcome to make me the person I am today.

I hope my story inspires you to believe in yourself and create the life that you truly deserve.

All my love Gem x

Disclaimer

This book is a memoir. It reflects the author's present recollections of experiences over time. Some names and characteristics have been changed, some events have been compressed, and some dialogue has been recreated.

"The queen of the North was born".

Tuesday 10th May 1983 I, Gemma Worth arrived into the world. Born in Macclesfield, Cheshire or as I like to call it the greatest place on earth …. "The North".

Eighteen months later came the arrival of my brother Ryan and the bond was formed.

For the next nine years it was just Mum, Dad, Ryan and I. I have so many wonderful memories, mainly with my Dad. Each weekend, weather permitting, Dad, Ryan and I would spend time at Manchester airport plane spotting. We would set off with our packed lunch and our little picnic chairs, full of excitement to see the planes taking off and landing and dreaming one day we would be able to fly a plane. Dad would have his "wireless" as he used to call it and tune in to the air traffic control. All of us had our own pair of binoculars and would mark down the plane registration numbers. Little did I know then that this weekly tradition would stick with me throughout adulthood. Another one of our weekly traditions was to spend Sunday's at my Grandmas [my Dads Mum] watching Bullseye on the TV with the biscuit tin. She was a typical Grandma, always feed us up with sugar before we went home.

My love of music is all down to my Dad. As soon as Mum was out, Dad would get out the LP's, always Status Quo, he would turn it up so loud Ryan, my Brother, and I would have our air guitars at the ready jumping from one sofa to another. Even now whilst writing this, I have a huge smile on my face. The memories I have with my Dad and Ryan will stick with me for a lifetime.

I remember Tuesday's was Mums giro day. Giro day we lived like kings for a day. We always had what we called a "picnic tea", it was the highlight of the week. Then on the other hand, the night before, Monday nights was our "peasant" tea night. We would cook whatever was left in the fridge or the freezer; you never knew what was going to end up on your plate. A turkey twizzler and a potato waffle usually accompanied by a tablespoon of bullet beans. Now I can just see the expression on your faces reading that. "Bullet Beans", let me explain. From our local supermarket Mum would buy the supermarkets own brand beans. The tin wrapper was white with blue stripes, two stripes to be exact. They were priced at nine pence a tin, and with that been said, our pantry was full from the floor up with these delightful tin beans. Ryan and I could not stand these beans and most tea times we would have a little game flicking them across the table at one another, resulting in a sore back side and the rest of the evening in our rooms. We always messed around at teatime flicking beans, peas or sweetcorn at each other. Ryan called sweetcorn yellow peas, and to this day I will never understand why he didn't call peas green peas! Due to these beans being so hard especially when we flicked them at each other, Ryan and I christened them Bullet Beans. If one of these beans caught you on the head you would certainly know about it. I have such fond memories with my younger brother.

Thinking about our little game has brought another fond memory to mind. Have you ever grabbed your quilts and slid down the stairs?

Ryan and I made this a daily ritual, we loved it but, at times it did not go according to plan and we would end up with carpet burns or in a heap at the bottom of the stairs crying. I sometimes wonder how we are both still alive.

Where we lived there was a farmer's field called Tinny Fields, we would spend hours and hours over the summer holidays making rope swings, jumping into the reservoir, at that age we were fearless. I always remember one time there was a herd of cows and Ryan and I thought it would be a good idea to poke the cows with sticks. I never knew that cows could run so fast. This one cow was not impressed with our constant prodding and poking, it made a sharp turn and started to run towards us, the rest of the herd then followed and before we knew it, we were being chased by ten cows. I remember being so scared. Ryan just did not care, he was fearless and brave, unlike me. We ran for our lives and it felt like miles over the fields and down to the canal. I hid under the bridge shaking and all I can remember was Ryan shouting from the bridge of the canal "Gemma you are a wimp" to which I replied, "Ryan I know, leave me alone". After I had calmed down from the cow chase, I stormed off home and told my Dad. But Dad was not impressed with what Ryan and I had done to the cows. I can remember feeling terribly upset that my Dad had shouted at me and sent me to my room. Half an hour later Ryan arrived home and he too was chastised and sent to his room. I can remember feeling terribly upset, not that I had done wrong but, because my Dad had shouted at me. I was a little angry too so, I packed my rucksack with my Barbie dolls and sneaked downstairs into the kitchen to get a bottle of water and some ten pence crisps, and I was gone.

Across from our house there was a park. I decided to run away to the park, not that I got very far. I was sat hiding in a metal tube that linked onto a slide. I remember in the distance hearing my Dad shouting "Gemma we know where you are". Silly me had always said to my dad that if I were ever homeless, I would sleep in this metal tube because the wind and rain would not get to me, so my Dad knew exactly where I was!

Ryan and I would always plan to run away, we would pack a bag and hide it in our wardrobes with the plan to wake up at 3am to sneak out the house, this never happened we were always too scared. We always wanted to go and stay with our Nana [My Mums Mum], she lived on the Moss Estate. She had a big house with two big gardens, we loved to stay at our Nana's house. She was a very firm woman but, also very loving, she had one of the looks that you just knew when to behave. I always remember on a Saturday night we would go and stay over; it was at the time that Noels House Party was airing on television (really showing my age now). We would always have a cooked dinner and we never messed around at Nana's table. Just like clockwork, 6pm after tea Grandad would go out to the local snooker centre, 11pm he would catch the last bus home. As he left for the snooker centre the ice cream van would come onto the street. Nana would always buy one for us, we would sit on the floor in front of the two-bar gas fire and watch Saturday night TV. Nana would always be knitting something. I even had a go myself at knitting, never did manage to get the hang of it. I remember Grandad saying to me once "by the time you can knit you will have made a jumper big enough for me. He was a big man over 6 feet tall and probably twenty stone and I can assure you he was not a man to be messed with, Ryan and I were scared to death of him.

Every morning at Nana's we would sit at the table for breakfast with cornflakes not the cheap brand we were used to at home, we had the best at Nana's. We ate like kings. We even had toast. At 11am each Sunday morning Nana would catch the bus to Mum's house. Whenever she was there, Nana would always clean our house from top to bottom and any decorating that needed to be done, my Nana did it. I loved my Nana. Whenever she was at our house it brought order and stability.

Before Nana made her journey back home, we would walk down to the local supermarket to get the reduced bread for my Mum. We walked back to the house like a pair of donkeys, bags packed over our arms. I was so embarrassed because, back then you were classed as poor on the estate if you were caught buying cheap items or if you shopped at budget supermarkets.

Now, I must tell you more about Grandma [my Dad's Mum]. Grandma was the total opposite to Nana. She was exceedingly small and frail; she wore a head scarf and had one of those old-fashioned shopping trolleys. She lived in a bungalow on the Weston Estate, she had lived in the same bungalow since I was born. It was tiny but so cosy. Ryan and I would play tennis on the front garden and we were always allowed to eat "rubbish" like cakes, biscuits and crisps. Grandma would let us do what we liked, no rules. A big contrast from being at my Nana's house. I remember sitting watching Bullseye, snooker and tennis. I would sit and draw cats with my Gran and I would name them all. Sadly, Mum did not like Dad's side of the family. Whenever she could, she would stop me going and this made my childhood incredibly sad at times. When I got the chance, I would sneak to

Grandma's house and if ever Mum called up at her bungalow, Grandma would lie and say she had not seen me. Grandma would always give me thirty-eight pence to get the bus back home and a pound for sweets. Now a pound back then in the nineties for sweets was a big deal. Sadly, Mum soon found out what I was doing and I was grounded for a very long time.

It wasn't long before life at home quickly changed. Mum and Dad had three further children and it became very apparent that the home was not a happy place. Dad was a bus driver at the time and I remember one particular night Mum and Dad having a massive argument. Dad had lost his job; he'd been caught drink driving whist at work. He was driving a double decker bus at the time and drove the bus under the train bridge in Macclesfield. The problem was the bus was too high to pass under the bridge. It was at this time I found out that my Dad was an alcoholic. In the past I had seen Dad steal the money Mum had left out to pay the milk man. Once I caught him stealing money from my piggy bank, he made some excuse and I believed him, just as any little girl would at thirteen. My Dad was my world, my hero.

Soon after the bus incident and Dad losing his job, he left our home and went to live with my Grandma. Mum was left with five children to look after, which quickly took its toll on her. You would expect most Mothers to be loving, maternal and supportive……. Well not mine. At thirteen I soon became the Mother figure to my siblings. Mum was going out all the time, getting drunk, bringing different men home with her. Fuelled with alcohol she would start "kicking off" throwing plates and cups at me, screaming and shouting, telling me I was nothing and never ever would be. Mum inflicted this abuse at me I believe because from preschool age I had developed a very bad stammer. I could not speak one word without my stammer. Starting school, I struggled when learning to read. At home I got no help. If I had difficulty with a word, I would just get abuse rather than help and encouragement. Mum would just yell abuse at me. I eventually became so nervous when reading it escalated into a full-blown speech impediment. As you've probably guessed, I was a prime target for being bullied at school. Even out of school I was scared, nervous and anxious all the time. I struggled to walk into a shop, use a phone or ask for help. This took over my life and made life extremely difficult for many years. I endured years of speech therapy but, that damn stammer stayed with me until I was in my late twenties.

Life was hard at home since Dad left. I remember when my younger sister was only a few weeks old Mum left all us kids on our own for two days. Being the eldest, I soon had to learn very quick how to look after a baby as well as the rest of the family.

I missed so much school but, back then in the nineties, schools were so much more relaxed if you did not attend, no school emails, phone calls, text or fines like there is today.

Arguments were always there at home. Mum would always "blow off the handle". I once asked Mum if I could go and see my Dad and Grandma. Well no one would have never expected the explosive argument that followed. I was just thirteen and because I wanted to see my Dad and Grandma, Mum went into a rage and kicked me out of my home. I had been made homeless by the woman that should be protecting me, loving me. All I wanted was to see my Dad and Grandma. Thirteen years old and out alone in the dark. I spent that night sleeping in West Park; I was too scared to tell my Dad or Grandma I had been kicked out. Eventually I was allowed to return back to the place I should have called home.

My Dad's alcoholism was now spiralling out of control. He no longer lived at Grandma's. He started to rent a room in a shared house. One particular night he was that drunk he fell and cracked his head open in the kitchen. I will never forget what day that was because the headlines that morning on the TV news was that Princess Diana had died. I visited Dad but, never told my Mum. I told her I was staying at my friend's house.

Due to the issues Dad brought, he soon lost the room in the house share. He had no alternative but to go back and live with my Grandma. Far from an ideal situation, she only had a one bedroomed bungalow but what could my Grandma do, this was her son. Grandma would find empty bottles of cheap whiskey thrown in the hedges at the side of her house. Dad always denied they were his empty bottles, he would constantly lie but, that's what alcoholics do, lying is just a part of the disease! Dad remained an alcoholic for many years and we slowly drifted apart. I had lost my hero, the first man I ever loved. I was heartbroken but, I believed there was nothing I could do to help him.

At home nothing ever changed, I would get kicked out for the slightest thing, begged to go back then I would be made to look after my siblings because that's what suited Mum. It was a vicious circle. Most Mothers are your role models, your "go to person", I never had that in my life. Mum began to self-harm in front of my brother and I. We witnessed things that no child should ever be subjected to. Both Ryan and I became a target for Mum. Nothing was ever good enough and being screamed and shouted at was now the norm in our life. We were never allowed to be children. I was always terrified to be around her. That was until I turned fifteen, everything changed. I rebelled; I would sneak out of the house at all hours of the night. School days I would hide out at a friend's house while her Dad was at work but, we always made sure we left her house before her Dad came home from work. To others it looked like we had been to school all day. School life was just as bad as being at home for me. The bullying continued because of my speech so, in the end I just never attended school. I missed all my exams and eventually I was kicked out of school.

In 1999 I experienced my first encounter of loss. My Nana passed away from her battle with cancer. She was the glue that I felt held our family together. I was extremely close to my Nana. I would spend most of my weekends at her house; I was her first granddaughter and secretly I knew that I was her favourite. Nana battled lung cancer for just over two years, I remember the day she asked me to shave her hair off due to the chemotherapy treatment. She was your typical northern Nana, no messing about and very straight talking. She was so brave and strong and that will always stay with me forever. One memory I will keep forever is sitting with her on the bed and she asked me to go to the wardrobe and pick her some nice clothes out for her funeral. Now at sixteen this was such a hard thing to do, but in a way, I am glad I did this for her. As hard as it was for me, how hard must this have been for my Nana? She always showed such bravery and strength, and I feel that she gave me the strength to become a strong independent woman later in my life. Shortly after Nana passed things really became unbearable at home. Mum spiralled out of control, which I never understood at the time. It was only when I lost a parent that I utterly understood the reasoning behind my Mum's actions. This didn't help things and Ryan soon became involved in crime. He was sent to a young offender's prison; little did I know then that this would be the start of his long and destructive road of crime and drugs.

It was the summer of 1999, I had now officially left school. I had no qualifications and was living on my mate's sofa. Life was well and truly rotten. I don't know how, but I managed to get a job at a local school cleaning in the afternoons earning sixty pounds a week. I thought I was the richest girl alive. As time went on, I managed to build bridges with Mum and was now living back at home.

Then I met my first boyfriend.

"The girl was in love".

I was only sixteen when I fell in love. I met him at the school I worked at. He was a lot older than me, thirty-one in fact. I was obsessed with him. As the saying goes…. If only I knew then, what I knew now.

Things were amazing as they always are at the start of any relationship however; I was a young naive sixteen year old girl, who really did not know any better. I would get dolled up and go out round Macclesfield town with my boyfriend. Back then it was one pound a pint in some of the pubs. I felt on top of the world. I was loved, being treated like an adult. It wasn't long before Mum kicked me out again. I had no alternative but to move in with my boyfriend. He lived in a shared house; he was separated, had two young children and was going through a messy divorce. The shared house was too small for us all, especially when he had his children at the weekend so, we decided to leave Macclesfield and move in with his Mother in New Mills, Derbyshire.

I was now seventeen and still working at the school cleaning. Things started to get strained. Living together and working at the same place we were just not getting on so, I left my job at the school and managed to get two jobs. One a cleaning job at the local gym and the other a part time job at a local shop in New Mills. But, as the months went on my boyfriend started to get jealous, and it escalated into drunken rages, this is when the abuse started.

I was scared to look in the direction of a man whenever we were out for fear of it "kicking off". He would call me fat and lots of other nasty things. My confidence was now at rock bottom. He would come in from work and cause an argument for no reason. The abuse got that bad he would burn me with cigarettes in my sleep, pin me to the bed and hit me as well as inflicting the most unimaginable things to me. This abuse went on for several years, until one day I found the courage to steal his car and drive back to Macclesfield. I turned up at Mum's house in a mess. I just wanted my Mum and after everything that had happened between us, she welcomed me back in the house with open arms.

I started to rebuild my life; I worked four jobs to pay the rent on a house. It felt like such an achievement. The house was a little two up two down, my brother's and sister's would come and stay over and even Dad would come and visit me. Sadly, it was not long before my dad used my house as a place to escape and drink. I had an optic in my kitchen with bottles of spirits which soon started to disappear. I realised my Dad was drinking again. When I confronted him, as always, he would deny it but, Ryan and I knew it was him. This went on for a few years and I chose to turn a blind eye to my Dad's drinking until enough was enough.

It was 2004 and my Mum had decided to move to Lancashire to run a pub. I made the decision to make this move with her. I started to work for my mum behind the bar and I met some amazing people. Things were good for a few months and as it always did, things started to turn sour very quickly. As well as working behind the bar for Mum, I also had a part time cleaning job. One day after I finished my cleaning job, I arrived home to find Mum and the rest of the family had gone, they had left that day. Not only had they gone but, there was a new landlord there behind the bar! I had to get my things and leave there and then. In a split second I had lost my home, my family and my job.

I went to stay with a friend and my life really deteriorated I started to drink heavily, party all weekend and generally not take care of myself. The drink and drugs became a big problem for me. I found myself getting involved with the wrong sort of people, spending what money I had on drugs. Things were so bad one Christmas, I sat with a pot noodle for my Christmas dinner. This was all I could afford. It got to the point where I had to choose whether to eat or put money on my gas and electric meter. Things really hit a very low point in my life. I started stealing from shops to feed myself. I really could not see a way out of this hole I had got myself into. I had no one,

Ryan was in jail again, my other siblings were living somewhere, I didn't know where, with Mum, I could not see a light at the end of this tunnel.

Things had to change and only I could change it. I woke up one day and decided this is the day. I started job hunting. After hours of sending CV's off to any available vacancies, at last I received a call back from a cleaning company. They had a contract with the local council where I was living. I attended the interview and was offered the job there and then and was asked to start on the Monday. I had such a feeling of relief. I started work on the Monday and the hours were 6am until 3pm. My job was to clean the recently vacated houses that the council owned. I was working alongside a guy that had worked cleaning for the council for many years. Most of the jobs we attended were relatively easy and straightforward. Full clean from top to bottom, all cupboards cleared and carpets taken up.

One day we were asked to clean a house in a known drug area of the town. Upon arrival we took our cleaning products and entered the property. To my dismay I have never, ever, encountered a scene like it in my life. I counted over one hundred used needles, rubbish bags piled high, human faeces alongside animal faeces. I could not believe what I was about to do.

It took us over nine hours to clear that house of the rubbish; we had to use specialist equipment for the used needles. That night I got back to my friend's house and I cried. I never, ever wanted to witness anything like that again. What made it so upsetting for me, was that children must have lived in the house because there were toys and a slide in the back garden, it broke my heart. The next day I decided that I needed go look for another job.

Weeks went by; I started to apply for pub manager jobs as I had the experience. One day a company contacted me offering me an interview. I went along and the interview I thought did not go well but, to my amazement a week later I received a call offering me the job. The problem was the pub and the job was down in Dartford, Kent. What did I have to lose? I accepted the job and I was on my way to live in Kent.

I started my new chapter in a new town and in the south of England. Now as a northerner, this came with its problems unfortunately. My north west accent stood out like a sore thumb and I made heads turn when I spoke. Most of the locals eventually got used to the Manchester tones in my accent and I made a lot of friends. But sadly, some of the locals did not take to me and my Manchester accent and I was subject to drunken abuse. I just took this on the chin, with my northern charm and with hard work I soon became a permanent fixture in the pub and I was offered the landlady position which was a great achievement. I became friends with one of the local's daughter, Linda. We were inseparable. We would go out after the pub was shut and plan trips away. One weekend we decided to go up to Newcastle. I always wanted to marry a Geordie lad, so I thought jokingly this was a perfect opportunity to find my husband to be. The road trip started. We were on our long drive to Newcastle. It was Christmas time and I remember Mariah Carey was playing. I burst out into song "all I want for Christmas is a "Geordie". We arrived in Newcastle and hit the town. As the night went on, we up met with a group of locals and were invited back to one of their houses. That night soon became a blur, we had no clue where we were. We woke up and left the party as if it was the walk of shame, although that was not the case. We flagged a taxi back to our hotel where everyone was sitting eating their breakfast and here was us, still in our going out clothes just arriving back from a night out. A quick shower and we were back out in the "toon" for breakfast. We headed up to St James Park or as I like to call this "the shrine". I was a huge Newcastle United fan, the only reason behind this was that my stepfather was from Sunderland and I wanted to put the cat amongst the pigeons and support Newcastle. What a fantastic stadium. Soon the weekend had finished and we were on our way back to Kent. Things were going great, life was good.

Today was one of those rare days. I had the day off work. Linda and I decided to go to a small local village for dinner. The pub we stopped at was called the Red Lion. A small village pub, absolute stunning place with a beautiful beer garden. It was a lovely sunny day so we decided to stay outside. I sat in the beer garden whilst Linda went to order our drinks and collect a menu. After a few minutes we decided what we wanted to eat and I went inside to order. I was not prepared for what happened next. I encountered the most shocking experience of my life. I had not spoken to my Mum for quite a long time and, to my horror, there she stood right there behind the bar. I had to take a second and third look. I froze. I was unsure what to do. After what seemed like ages, I gathered myself, walked up to the bar and just said "Hello Mum". Of all the places in the world my Mum could have disappeared to when she left Ryan and I a few years prior, she had to move to Kent. You really could not write this, so to speak. There was a very awkward silence at first, then we made small talk and had a small conversation, then my stepdad made an appearance. On this, I went back outside to Linda and relayed what had just happened, in shear shock and disbelief she thought that I was joking. Who could blame her? It sounded too farfetched to be true, but it was. After long consideration and a lot of heartfelt thoughts being the person I am, I decided to let the past lie and try and build a new relationship with Mum. Things started off great but, as always this only lasted for a short period of time.

A few months later the owner of Mum's pub, the Red Lion, contacted me and asked if I would be interested in moving to Ipswich to run a pub. Nothing to lose really so I drove over to Ipswich and had a look at the pub. It was a small pub with a functional kitchen situated close to the River Orwell. This would always have passing trade from tourists I thought to myself so, I decided to take the chance and make the move to Ipswich. I loved it here. It was 2006, the year of the World Cup. Being a big football fan, I decorated the pub to celebrate the World Cup, gave out free food and totally turned this pub around. The pub was packed out. It was becoming apparent that I had a real talent on turning pubs around and I was in my element. I loved the hard work and loved making new friends.

During the time I was in Ipswich there was a serial murderer on the loose. The Ipswich Strangler, who had murdered five victims and one happened to be down the road from my pub.

This was a very frightening time as I ran the pub on my own. Of all the places to move to and run a pub, I chose the same place as a serial killer! The police presence in the village was phenomenal. I chose not to leave the pub unless it was necessary. Thankfully the murderer was apprehended in the December and Ipswich soon started to return to normal.

The following year, 2007, my Mum and my stepdad were offered to buy some of the pubs off the current owner. Worryingly one of these pubs happened to be mine and another one in Norfolk. They accepted the offer and now I had "new landlords" so to speak. At first nothing changed. Then one day, my Mum and stepdad decided they wanted me to transfer over to the pub in Norfolk, which I was not happy about. I refused the offer and told them I did not want to leave the pub I was running. Unbeknown to them I decided to nip over to Norfolk to look at their other pub. It was a beautiful bed and breakfast with a big garden and kitchen to offer food to customers.

One night my Mum and stepdad came over to Ipswich and after Mum had had a few drinks, all kicked off. She started to shout abuse at me in front of everyone. I felt so embarrassed. As the past has taught me, Mum was never good when she drank, a horrible drunk you could say. We got into a massive argument and she punched me from over the bar. My stepdad then told me I had to leave. I was kicked out of the pub. I had to leave that night. Luckily for me one of the customers put me up at their house. After a few weeks I decided to go and confront Mum as someone had told me she was in Ipswich visiting the new landlord they had put in my old pub. When I arrived, my stepdad came to me and asked if I could speak with Mum and sort things out, which surprised me as he was the one that kicked me out in the first place! Reluctantly and more stupidly I agreed. Surprisingly following our talk, Mum offered me the landlady job at the Norfolk pub. I thought about it and decided really, I didn't have any other options, I couldn't stay on the customers settee forever. I had no money nor any other job, so here I was again on the move to another new area.

Now let me set the scene. Beautiful Norfolk countryside and I was the only pub in the village alongside a post office and a corner shop. The nearest town was seventeen miles away called Kings Lynn. I was not too far from Cromer and the picturesque Swaffham village.

This pub was a far cry from my usual habitat. I am a town girl from an estate. I found myself in this beautiful Norfolk countryside but, at the same time felt very isolated. I opened the doors as my first day as the new landlady feeling incredibly nervous, as I really did not know how the locals would react to me, a northerner from a council estate!

As always talk in the village of a new landlady spread around and customers began to come into the pub, more so to be nosey I imagine. I was no stranger to this with my previous experience running pubs. The locals were lovely, bookings were coming in for the bed and breakfast, and the lunch time trade was picking up. It was a lot to take on with the bed and breakfast. There were nine rooms to take care of and as I had only just started this job, I only employed one member of staff. I soon became the chef, the landlady and the housekeeper. I was extremely tired but I carried on seven days a week juggling all my roles. Meanwhile back in Ipswich there was a new landlord, John, a guy from Liverpool. He was your typical Liverpudlian, friendly, outgoing. We hit it off straightway when we had a team meeting at my pub in Norfolk, we exchanged numbers and we formed a good friendship.

I decided to take a rare day off work and drive over to Ipswich to see all my old customers and my new found friend. The day was good, lots of catching up was done and I had a really enjoyable day. As the day came to an end I drove back to Norfolk in really good spirits. I'd enjoyed my trip so much, seeing all my old customers, reminiscing. I decided to make it a regular outing so, once a week I drove over to Ipswich. I needed a break more often, especially a break from Norfolk. The pub I ran was stunning but the country life really was not for me. I love the hustle and bustle of a town or city, access to shops twenty-four seven and being close to people. My weekly drive to Ipswich was my escape to reality.

Unfortunately, my weekly break was short lived. Mum was controlling and she didn't like me visiting Ipswich and the friends I had made. I should have learnt by now that if Mum doesn't like or agree with something, then she will do her best to get her way. Again, like the incident in the Ipswich pub, Mum created an argument in the pub in Norfolk, this time in front of all the customers. Having a manipulating and very clever Mum, she soon turned this into a situation so that I looked the bad person, all because I was meeting old friends once a week and Mum disagreed! The situation soon turned into a full-blown altercation, even one of the locals decided to get involved. You probably guessed by now, I came off the worst and once again I was kicked out of my home and my job.

This time I had nowhere to go, my only option was to sleep in my car. I'm embarrassed to say, I stole a quilt from one of the guest rooms but, I had no other means of keeping warm. I gathered my personal belongings and left. That night my car was my bed it was all I had. I was homeless, no job and nowhere to go. I was angry with myself, again I had let my guard down with Mum and I had been hung out to dry for the tenth time in my life.

The following day I contacted John in Ipswich and explained what had happened. He kindly agreed to let me stop at the pub but, we had to be very careful that Mum didn't find out.

I had to act quickly, I needed a job and a home. The only way I knew how to get both was to run another pub. I went to the local library in Ipswich and started to apply for all the pub manager jobs available. My luck was in, at last. Within a day I had a call back with an interview for a pub in Wrexham. Not where I wanted to move to but, I was in a desperate situation. I spoke with the area manager who made it clear that they were looking for a management couple due to the location of the pub in Wrexham. Not to be discounted I had to think quick, very quick. I asked John if he would like to take this pub on with me as a management couple. Without any hesitation he agreed. He was disgusted in the way Mum had treated me and he wanted a clean break from Ipswich and from working for her and my stepdad. That night he packed his car up ready then the following morning he left the pub keys with a neighbour along with a note fastened to the pub door. Then we were on our way to Wrexham. I would have loved to be a fly on the wall when my Mum and Stepdad found the note. We arrived at Wrexham, ready for the next new adventure. Situated on the main High Street along with other pubs, it was in a prime location. I was excited another move, another new town and another new chapter. We met with the area manager and he showed us around the place. The upstairs was not in a good state and the area manager knew this. He gave me a thousand pounds to buy the essential items that were needed.

It was December 2007 and one of the busiest times in the pub world. Things were good, the pub was making good money, the wages were great, what could go wrong?

The Christmas period was good but, New Year's Eve as you can imagine was a money maker. That night was a success, we'd taken over four thousand pounds. It was around two o'clock in the morning by the time I managed to get to bed. It was my job to clean the pub and open up, John had agreed to do the afternoon shift. So, I set my alarm for nine o clock that morning. Nine o'clock and my alarm went off. I was so tired from the previous night's New Year's celebrations but, I remember thinking to myself the wage next week will be incredible. I will finally be able to say I have some money in the bank. With that I crawled out of bed, showered, got dressed then headed off to turn off the alarm for the pub. Confused I realised that the alarm was disarmed? I knew that the alarm was set the previous evening when I went to bed. I went downstairs thinking John must be downstairs, he must have turned it off. I arrived downstairs but the pub was in darkness, I turned the lights on, the pub was empty. I was now extremely confused and without thinking anything more about it concluded it must be me, I must have made a mistake and not armed the alarm the previous night. I went about my chores, cleaned the pub and got everything ready for opening. Being New Year's Day, the banks were closed and no banking could be done however, I had to complete the paperwork for the previous night's takings and phone them through to the area manager. Unknown to me my biggest nightmare was now awaiting me. I went back upstairs to the safe only to find it empty, all of the takings had gone. I knew hand on heart that I had put them in the safe the night before myself. Panic started to hit me. I searched the pub, my bedroom, even though I knew I'd locked them away I still searched everywhere. Then the realisation kicked in, I went to John's room to find he and all his belongings had gone. I quickly ran outside to check if his car was in the carpark. No it had gone. The sick realisation, the feeling of betrayal hit me like a thud. I will never forget that feeling. I sat and cried, I did not know what to do. I soon realised I had no choice but to contact the area manager and inform him of what had happened. Try and explain how John, who I thought was my friend, had taken all the money from the safe and left in the early hours of that morning. I contacted the area manager then the police. The police arrived and I gave a statement of the events. The area manger had now arrived and as you can imagine he was not impressed with the situation. The police left but, to my horror after a few hours they returned and arrested me on suspicion of theft. I was taken to the police station in Wrexham and placed in a holding cell. This was the first time I had ever been arrested. The whole situation was a terrifying experience but, at the same time a very strange one. I'd been arrested for something I'd not done. Placed in a cell but, I was still in possession of my handbag which had my mobile phone in! I remember thinking to myself, I am sure they do not do this on the television. From my cell with my mobile phone, I started texting Paul a friend in Macclesfield. We had been friends since school, when Paul received the text, he could not believe what he was reading.

A few hours later I was interviewed then bailed pending further investigation. The police along with the area manager truly believed I was part of this theft, which I was not. I was terrified and thought that I was going to jail. I left the police station and went to collect my belongings from the pub. During my time in the cell texting Paul, I had arranged for me to go and stay over in Macclesfield with him. Once again, I was homeless and without a job. I packed my car with all my worldly goods and drove to Macclesfield to stay with Paul in his pub on the estate where I was born. I helped out behind the bar to pay my way for staying there. Being the girl that I am it wasn't long before I managed to get myself a job. A small job I admit but it was a job. I started as a cleaner at a local school.

A month passed and it was time to answer bail in Wrexham. I was so scared. Terrified in fact, very nervous and felt sick. At the police station I was made to wait for over two hours before being asked into the interview room. All charges were dropped against me! I couldn't believe what I was hearing but I can tell you the relief was immense. I drove back to Macclesfield in disbelief I knew that I had a lucky escape. I also knew I had learnt the hard way, trusting John who I thought was a friend was a big mistake. I told myself I would never let my guard down again.

A few months had passed, I was working three jobs but I missed being my own boss and I missed running my own pub. I knew I was good at running pubs so I started applying for pub manager jobs. My determination paid off and I was offered a mangers job in Peterborough. There was only one problem, a big one at that. I'd heard on the great vine that my Mum and stepdad had moved not far from Peterborough. But I thought to myself I cannot let that stop me. I accepted the job in Peterborough and once again I moved to start another new chapter.

The Cross Keys, my new home, was on London Road which led directly to Peterborough football ground. I had a big challenge on my hands, the pub had been run into the ground by the previous mangers, but that didn't deter me, I was up for this challenge. The Cross Keys had a kitchen, admittedly it hadn't been used for a while so I thought "why not". I put a menu together and started to serve food in the afternoon and in the evening. I interviewed for two staff for the bar so I could concentrate on the food side of the business. The football was a crowd puller so I advertised the football every weekend and offered free food on some of the football matches to entice new customers. It worked. I was working very hard and it paid off.

The takings doubled in the first few weeks. Next, I introduced music events Friday and Saturday nights and quiz nights in the week. Within a few months I was making over two thousand pounds per week in wages! I worked an eighteen-hour day some days but I loved the hard work, I had a purpose. I made friends and the pub gained a good name in the town. In 2008 Peterborough football club were promoted to league one and believe me that day the pub was so busy. It had a fantastic atmosphere, the customers loved it. Later that night a group of lads walked in the pub, to me they were just local lads, which they were. However, it soon became apparent that the Peterborough Football Club players had just walked into my pub to celebrate their promotion. The news travelled around the town fast, my pub was now at its maximum capacity. Luckily for me, part of the licence condition being so close to the football ground was that I had security staff on my doors every weekend.

One of the players approached me and asked if the players could go behind the bar and pour drinks for the customers, he gave me a five hundred pounds for the pleasure and they took over the bar. I can't describe what it was like, to say the atmosphere was amazing is an understatement. There was no trouble and the customers were drinking and talking to the players, even the local paper turned up to take pictures. My pub was firmly on the map in Peterborough City. Sadly, with all this attention came yet more heartache.

I know I took a chance moving here with my Mum and stepdad living nearby but, I couldn't let that ruin my opportunity of making something of my life. However, I was not expecting them to ever find out that I lived in Peterborough. The local paper had put pictures of the football night along with my picture and name, they saw the review.

The landline rang, I answered and to my shock it was my stepdad. I was taken aback but I continued to take the call. Even though I had promised myself never to let my guard down again I did and I fell into the trap and let them back in to my life.

My stepdad had a gambling problem, he had had this addiction for years. He would gamble, owe people lots of money, build up debt then move on. My Mum and stepdad would move areas so much. They would leave during the night due to money he owed to people. Naively, I lent Mum money which, looking back was one of the worst mistakes I ever made. I was in my twenties but I was still very naïve. I was now a successful manager of a well-known pub in Peterborough and with all my hard work I now, for the first time in my life, had money, I was very comfortable. I was single with no children, the only people I could spend my money on was my family. Because I'd now formed yet another relationship with my family, I began taking my younger sister out for day trips. I would spoil her with gifts, she was only six and she was my favourite person, I loved her so much. My stepdad soon saw this situation as an opportunity for his benefit. He asked for money on several occasions which, without hesitation I agreed and loaned him the money. That was me all over. I had the money and I am a generous kind person, silly in this case I can now see but, I always believed if I have something and you need it, you can have it. It still is my motto in life. It soon became apparent that my Mum and stepdad were jealous of my success. They made stories up and told many lies about me all around Peterborough, then they stopped me having a relationship with my little sister. One day I was working at the pub when someone started throwing eggs at the pub window. Looking outside I could see it was my young brother, he was only ten years old. Incidents like this became a regular occurrence and things soon escalated when, one day I received a phone call from the area manager of the pub saying that they had received several complaints about me from the locals. I knew who was behind this but I had no proof, my life had now become a living hell. On another occasion I woke up to find that my car had been vandalised, scratched all down one side. I called the police but sadly because my car was parked out of reach of the cameras in the car park there was no evidence of who the criminal was.

My Mum and stepdad had now taken over the running of a pub just down the road from me which was owned by the same people who owned my place. All I could think was here we go again, yet another move to sabotage my life, they tried everything to ruin my reputation. I had so many nights of my windows been egged. They even got my younger brother to run into the pub and throw shop bought stink bombs into the pub. It was their way of emptying my pub. No customers – no business. This was only the start of it all. One night the pub was broken into and my car keys were taken and my car stolen. My car was later found burnt out, the police had no leads and no evidence on who may have committed this crime, but I had other ideas. I could not cope with anymore and decided to leave without notice. I contacted my friend from Lancashire to ask if I could move back in for a while. I explain all that had happened and said I just need to get away. That night I packed up my car up as I planned to leave early the following morning. I completed all the paperwork and left the pub clean and tidy and locked safely away the takings. I left through the side door of the pub, closed the door and posted the keys back through. I was on my way to Lancashire.

During my journey, I received a call from an unknown number. It was the police, they wanted to speak to me on allegations of a theft at my pub. I was confused, I explained that I had left the pub, all the money and paperwork was locked away in the safe. Apparently, my stepdad had discovered the main door of the pub open and unlocked and contacted the police who discovered the pub had been burgled. This news soon went around the town and for me things were not looking good. I made my way back to Peterborough to speak to the police. Little did I know that when I arrived at the police station I would be arrested and put in a cell for the night. I was charged with theft from the pub and bailed for a month. After the months bail was up, I drove back to Peterborough to the police station. Within five minutes a police officer escorted me into a room. I nervously sat down, where to my astonishment the officer proceeded to informed me all the charges had been dropped. I was in total shock, although I knew I was innocent.

I knew that the way I had left the pub the evidence surrounding the theft pointed the finger at me. Shocked and in disbelief I quickly asked the police officer did they have a suspect? He just informed me that they could not make any comment at this time. With that, I was allowed to leave. I drove back to Lancashire to start yet another chapter in my life even though Lancashire was the last place I wanted to be. With all the previous situations I'd experienced there I felt like I was stepping back in life and all I wanted was to move forward.

A few months passed and I received a text from someone I knew in Peterborough. Of all the texts to receive this one was to inform me that my stepdad had been arrested and charged with theft from my pub. He had tried to set me up with the theft. To say I was shocked again is an understatement, I could not believe it. From that day I made myself a promise. I promised myself that I would never have any further relationship with my Mum or my stepdad again, and that promise still stands to this day. I have had no contact with them at all since I left Peterborough. Enough was enough, I had in effectively divorced my own Mum.

So, yet again I found myself back to square one. I needed a job and fast, and I knew that I could run pubs, but I was desperate, I was willing to do any kind of work.

Things started to look up for me. This particular day I went to my local and the landlord asked if I wanted a few hours work. I "immodestly" jumped at the offer and said yes. I was desperate. I needed money to survive but, most importantly I did not want to end up going down the wrong path again like I had previously. The work soon became full time and I loved it. I loved it that much and proved myself again that, in 2009 I became the new landlady of The Queens in Accrington; I was running my own pub again. Another new chapter of my life had begun. It wasn't easy, this pub by far was one of the hardest challenges I had. When you take over any new pub all the locals come in to see who the new landlady or landlord is, this always comes with its own trouble. The local's customers that had previously been banned from the pub made their appearance and it was not long before I had fights breaking out.

It was time for me to begin my own list of barred customers. After months of hard work and many late nights the pub began to turn around for the better. With my previous experience I knew how to get customers in the pub. I began to introduce entertainment at the weekends and promoted the football with free food on match days.

Unfortunately, not all my days (and nights) were great. One night a serious argument broke out between a couple, I had no alternative but to remove them and tell them they were barred. The next day the windows of the pub were smashed, then a few hours later the woman I had barred the previous night came into the pub causing a disturbance. The incident soon became physical and a few other locals became involved. That night I ended up in hospital with broken ribs and a nasty cut on my head. I remember thinking to myself, the pub is my home and I had nowhere else to go but, I need to take a few days off work. I asked my staff to run the pub for the time I needed to recover. After a few days I returned to work, the staff were amazing they worked all the hours they could to support me. After a few months I was fully recovered, the pub was doing great and I had not had any more altercations.

I became good friends with a girl who worked for me, Ruth and our friendship blossomed, we became inseparable. She soon became my bar manager. Ruth was extremely good at her job and the customers loved her; things were great. A year went by and the pub was making a good profit and my area manager was happy with the progress I had made with the pub.

Now, like most pubs and clubs sometimes a friendly lock in is one of the perks of the job. This particular night we decided to let our hair down and with Ruth and her boyfriend we had a lock in. It was a good night, we had the juke box on, we danced and the drink was flowing. Around 3am it was time to finish up and time for bed, Ruth and her boyfriend went home. It was around 10am that morning when I woke up, got showered and dressed ready to clean the pub and open up for midday. After everything was done and the pub was ready for opening, I went upstairs to cash up and go to the bank. As I opened the safe it was like deja vu. To my horror the takings had gone, history was repeating itself. I tried franticly to gather my thoughts; my mind was in overdrive. The only people who had been in the pub the night before when I did the cashing up were Ruth, her boyfriend and myself. I searched high and low for the money, I don't know why because deep down I knew where the money should be and deep down, I had an idea what had happened to it. The only explanation was one or both of them had taken the money. I contacted Ruth but the conversation turned very nasty. She turned up at the pub with her boyfriend and she attacked me from over the bar and I had no option but to call the police. What I believed was a true friendship, it had gone, it was over in a split second, I found it hard to believe what had happened. I closed the pub that day and contacted my area manager. As you can imagine that was a hard phone call to make, my area manger arranged to see me the next day. The police came and they took my statement. The money was never recovered and to the best of my knowledge no one has ever been charged with the theft. To me, it remains a mystery to this day. To keep my job and my home, the hardest thing for me was I had to repay all the money that was stolen. I did this out of my weekly salary and by doing this it had an adverse effect on my income. I had no alternative but to reduce my staffing hours but, I did it, I struggled through and paid back all the stolen money to the company. I will be honest, at that point I was ready to leave, to give up, I felt defeated but, what could I do, the pub was my home as well as my job. I felt very isolated and alone, how was it possible to feel so alone in a room full of people? Then things move in mysterious ways as they say and as if the universe was listening to me this guy walked in. Tall, dark and handsome, covered in tattoos and what I can only describe as "full of himself", but I loved that. Move over loneliness, now started another chapter in my life. Within weeks I had fallen in deeply love. He was a single father of three children but that didn't deter me. I took on his children as though they were my own and we were married 21st May 2010, exactly nine months after first meeting. We had an amazing time together, always laughing and joking, we started working together and things were perfect, we were inseparable.

He even taught me how to play the guitar. The dream team in my eyes, untouchable and unstoppable and I adored him like no other. A few months passed and we decided to leave the pub and start a new life as a family. We moved to a council estate and set up home. We did not have a lot. In terms of money we were on benefits, second hand furniture furnished our home but that didn't matter, it was home and for the first time in my life I was happy.

Every Saturday we would have a bet on the football, our treat. All we could afford was fifty pence accumulators, but it didn't matter it was the highlight of my week. Every Saturday morning at 10 am we would walk down to the betting shop, place our bets and, in anticipation, wait to see what our return would be. If the twenty-fold accumulator actually won, we would then go to the local super market and buy cheap crisps and a few cans of cheap beer, maybe treated ourselves to a pot noodle. Honestly, we had very little but these were the best times of my life and I will never forget them as long as I live. Just goes to show you don't need money to have a good time and make lasting memories. However, as time went on, I soon began to realise that behind the laughs and the good times there were dark times also.

Now all marriages have their fair share of highs and lows. I was in a dream, madly in love and when we got married, I did not know that I was six weeks pregnant nor did I know that my husband had a drug addiction. Hard to believe I know but I did not know he was a drug addict. I was now faced with making the hardest decision of my life, not to go through with the pregnancy. How could I bring a baby into this kind of world? I was already Mum to three children, with no money, living with a drug addict who now had become violent towards me. That hard decision will stay with me for the rest of my life and I will always regret not being as strong as I am now. Sadly, things did not end there. One day I had a knock on the front door and there stood two men demanding money for an unpaid debt. We had no alternative but to raise the money. Most of the televisions in the house, the guitar I had bought him as a wedding gift, all sold on to a local shop to pay off this debt.

But that didn't stop him all the money we received in benefits went on drugs. I remember one day I had just £2.50 to my name. The kids were hungry and I was desperate. I went down to the local supermarket and bought a pack of cheap chicken and vegetable pies, a packet of mashed potato that you mixed with water, a tin of cheap peas and tub of gravy granules just so the children had a meal. The two of us never ate. I stood in the checkout queue in the supermarket and tears rolled down my face, I couldn't believe what my life had become. We had to beg, borrow and steal just to get by. Things were so bad that if I did eat, it was the norm for me to only have one meal a day. This continued for years and I could not see an end in sight. All I could think was I was married and I believed very much in love, what else could I do? Eventually our marriage ended up in a very toxic place and I will be the first to admit it was all not all one sided. I did start to fight back and hit him. I cannot sit here and tell you it was all him, it wasn't. I had to fight back. I had three beautiful children that I needed to protect, I brought these children up as my own and to this day I still do. They all call me Mum and I still believe we had some great times. In 2010 we decided to move to Derbyshire and at that time little did I know that this decision was the best move in my life. We took over the running of a local pub in a small friendly village called Clay Cross, just outside Chesterfield in Derbyshire. We ran the pub for the next three years and made some wonderful friends. One in particular is my dear friend Kirsty, who would become a very important part of my life.

When we arrived at our new home, for a local pub it was very run down and was not doing well financially. I knew it was going to be a hard road but I was ready for this next challenge. The first night we had to check into a local hotel because the living accommodation was only what I can describe as vile, no carpets, rubbish piled high and accommodating many fleas. The brewery brought in professional cleaners to make it habitable. A few weeks later I had made it a home. I soon started to form friendships with the locals but, back then my husband stuck out like a sore thumb. He soon started to upset some of the locals luckily, everyone seemed to love me. I was not shy to work, I did not employ a cleaner. I have always said "do not ask anyone to do a job that you are not prepared to do yourself" and I have always lived by that. I worked hard and soon turned this little pub around, takings were up and life seemed good. I always knew how to run a pub; I had gained many years of experience. I had moved all over the country, met all walks of life and gained valuable life experience along the way. The skills I had learnt during my managerial times gave me the confidence to do anything, confidence to run my own business.

I employed few members of staff, one being the friend who would be the one person who would play a massive part of my life as I would hers, Kirsty. Ten years down the line we have gone through just about everything: grief, childbirth, miscarriage, marriages, divorces, highs and lows you name it …. Everything. I truly believe in the saying, you can find a sole mate in a friend, and that is what I have.

The pub life was good for a few years, the normal stresses of life, the school run, paying the bills, the good times, holidays and city breaks away. But as time went on, drinking played a big part of my husband's life and the violence between us started again. The turning point in my life came during one violent argument that broke out upstairs. Kirsty ran up just as I had a knife in my hand ready to use on my husband. I'm ashamed to admit what I was ready to do but, that was the wakeup call for me. Thank God she was there. It wasn't long before another argument that soon turned into a fight, this time it wasn't upstairs, it happened behind the bar in front of a pub full of people. As you can imagine the customers were far from impressed and soon after that the takings dropped. We finally made the decision to leave the pub later that year.

We stayed in Clay Cross and moved into a lovely rented three bedroomed house. Both of us got a job and started to work on our new life at our new home. But sadly, it wasn't long before things became violent again. After a night out we started to fight and argue. This time it was worse than any other time we had fought, all three children witnessed the fight and it began to get physical. I tried my best to fight back but it was in vain. The last thing I remember is my face being hit against the kitchen cupboard door. I woke up on the floor in a pool of blood with a nasty cut to my head. The children had already rung for an ambulance and the police. According to the children he had kicked me repeatedly in my stomach whilst I was unconscious. I don't know how but I managed to get up off the floor and left the house. I went to my brother's flat just around the corner. He got a towel for my head and he also called an ambulance. I was taken to hospital where they stitched up the wound to my head. The police arrived at the hospital and wanted me to give a statement. I refused to do this. I knew it was wrong what he had done but, I did not want to get him arrested, after all I still loved him! Soon after I came out of hospital, we had a visit from social services who raised genuine concerns for the children's safety. After a few meetings they were satisfied the children were at no risk and the case was closed. As the years went on, we started to lead separate lives. Our relationship was great when things were good but, toxic when things were not. We were both head strong and both had explosive personalities and we clashed at times but there was no question of the love between us and that is what kept us together for the next ten years.

Happy birthday Ryan I love u more than u will ever know 😂😂😂

"The day it changed"

10th April 2014, the day my life changed forever; my dear Dad passed away after battling cancer. I cannot describe the pain I had, it felt like a light had gone off inside me. I tried to turn that light back on many times but it never shone as bright any more. I cannot sit here and say it was all good with him because it was far from it. In the past he stole from me, he lied and disowned me for years. He put the drink first, but honestly, I knew he was sorry. The hardest thing for me was sitting watching him deteriorate. He tried to apologise for all his wrongs but, I just said to him "Dad it's ok, I love you". My dad was the first man I had ever loved, my world had now well and truly fallen apart. This was not my first encounter with loss by 2014. I now had no grandparents, I had lost them all but, as much as I loved my grandparents this was my Dad, the pain and hurt was unbearable. My Dad was gone.

He was a huge Stoke City fan. City was his life and I remember before he passed away, I told him "one day Dad, our name will be shown around that ground". He just laughed and replied "I hope so Gemma".

Now, this is how I made that promise reality. Go back to 2013 when I was still the landlady of a pub in the village. The owners of the pub decided we all had to become self-employed and so we hired an accountant. The fees were ridiculously excessive, so I thought to myself I may as well try to do this myself. I surprised myself, I loved it and decided to enrolled on an accounting course at college. This is the girl who got kicked out of school without any qualifications and here I was finding a love for accountancy! Within the first four weeks of my course, I had a VAT exam, it fell the day after Dad's funeral. To this day I cannot tell you anything about that day and that exam but, I had passed it 100%. That is when I knew I was destined for bigger and better things. This put things into perspective and I decided to turn all my pain and grief into something positive.

That night Kirsty and I were walking through the village and there was this little shop selling baby clothes. I turned to Kirsty and said "one day that will be my office", she said "babe, I hope so". Three years later, studying weekends, going to university twice a week after work and with a university degree under my belt, I finally gained my accountancy qualification. My husband said "one day you will have all the self-employed people around on your books" and really, I need to thank him for putting that out into the universe because it certainly came true.

In 2017 I had secured a job at a local accountancy firm; I worked in payroll and soon was promoted to head of pensions. During this time, I had set up a little office working from home and I was slowly gaining clients month by month but nowhere near enough to make it a full-time job. I decided to set up a social media page and advertise my accountancy business. I chose the business name Hayes Worth and Stone. This was created with: Hayes my married name, Worth my maiden name and Stone for Stone Roses my favourite band.

In August 2017 I was about to go on holiday for two whole weeks to Florida. It was my last day at work before going and I was just about to leave when I was called into the office. Someone had seen my social media page and informed the managing partners. Apparently, part of my contract was that I was not allowed to engage in any other accountancy services. My employment was terminated there and then! Not a lot I could do really at that point so I still went on holiday. My life was really taking a backward step now because this much awaited dream holiday turned out to be the worst holiday of my life. It was there in Florida that I realised my marriage was well and truly over, the holiday that I had worked so hard to pay for. We had an altercation on International Drive in Florida, one of the main highways in the sunshine state. The following day I was told by the very man I had loved and forgiven so many times he was not happy and he didn't love me anymore. He said he had not loved me for many years.

This hurtful revelation from him hit me hard; I was completely shocked. We still had another week here in Florida and, even though things were far from right, I tried very hard to make the best of this bad situation. I was so alone I just needed someone to talk to and remember calling Kirsty back in England. I was devastated by what had happened on what should have been the holiday of a lifetime.

Life was throwing everything at me. I returned to England only to find out my stepdaughter was pregnant. She was fifteen. I had decided I had no choice but to stay in this marriage and support her. With all this going on I knew I had a big decision to make, make a go at my little business I started at home or find another job and go back to working for an employer. The following week, after the initial shock of my stepdaughter being pregnant, I was walking through the village and there in front of me was the little shop. The same little shop four years ago I said would be my office, it was advertised for rent. After some investigation I found out the shop was owned by the pub next door. Excitement built up inside. I knew the landlord so, with my fingers crossed and my heart thumping, I walked in and enquired about the shop. To my delight and surprise he threw the keys at me and said its yours.

Little did I know what would happen next.

"The boss Was born".

18th February 2018 I opened the door to what would be my haven, my happy place, and unbeknown to me then, the start of my empire.

The décor was something to be desired and I knew I had to get straight to work but then I realised I had no full-time job. All I had were the few clients from working at home and I was skint! I asked a friend's brother if he could lend me a £1000, which thankfully he did. I asked around friends if they would help me decorate and all of them agreed. I stood in the middle of this small office, I looked around and thought to myself "what I have done", then I just thought of my Dad and a wave of determination came over me. The decision of the colour scheme was easy, red and white, a tribute to my late father's beloved Stoke City FC. I'd also had a dream from being a little girl of one day going to New York City so, I decided to buy a big canvas of the Brooklyn Bridge as a visual goal that one day I would stand on that bridge. I wanted my office to stand out and reflect my personality. If you've not guessed by now, I am far from your typical looking accountant. I am covered in tattoos, all of which tell a story of my life and lessons and express to me what I've been through. I probably swear and drink too much so, all in all just not that typical accountant girl (so people would say).

I decide to organise an open day, a grand event and with the powers of social media I created a buzz. Four weeks passed and the open day was here, Saturday 10th March 2018. Hundreds of people turned up to wish me well. What a day and night it was and to be completely honest I cannot remember going home that night.

Monday came and I was open for business.

With my down to earth attitude, some social marketing and through word of mouth I soon took on client after client, within my first year I had signed up over 50 clients. I worked every weekend and late nights for months to get my business off the ground. I was determined, motivated and always thinking of new ways to sign up new clients. Honestly, I truly felt that my best asset for sales was myself. I have always stayed true to who I am and where I came from, I never pretend to be something I am not, and the clients love that.

A really good friend who also happens to a client of mine introduced me to a lady in Manchester. With my husband for company, I travelled over to Manchester to meet my new potential client. On meeting with her we immediately hit it off and I now had signed up my first client in Manchester, which was always a dream of mine. Following our meeting my husband and I walked through Fallowfield. I looked up and saw my next dream. "You see that building," I said to him, "that will be my next office one day." He turned to me and said "don't be daft", to which I responded "ok love" he hated it when I called him love and that was my way of saying I'll show you.

Maybe it was jealousy of my growing success or something else I don't know, but that night things really got bad and we ended up fighting on Piccadilly Gardens. With this and another incident to follow it started to hit home; my marriage was definitely coming to its end. December 2018 after we had had a night out, I was sitting eating a pot noodle when he started to kick off. A serious argument broke out and I tried to diffuse the situation by going upstairs to bed, but it didn't stop him. He followed me upstairs and pinned me to the bed. The next thing he was sinking his teeth into my face. Thankfully we had my brother staying at our house that night, he'd recently separated from his partner. Lucky for me he was there, he rushed into our room and pulled my husband off me and took him out of the room. It wasn't over, he came rushing back into the room straight for me, without thinking I reached for the pot noodle at the side of me and threw it at him causing him burns from the hot water. I was terrified so I went into my son's bedroom and spent the night there. The following morning my son begged me not to leave, but my mind was made up, I could not continue to be in this situation as I feared that before long one of us would be seriously hurt. I packed my bags of a few personal belongings and walked out of my home and my marriage of ten years, enough was enough. Years of physical abuse had taken its toll on me mentally and physically even though I am not completely blameless in some of the situations, but I knew for my safety and sanity I had to leave.

I went to stay with a friend who lived on the same street when realisation hit me. I had just a few of my personal belongings, I had left my whole life in the house, pictures of my Dad and Grandmother. I'd hit another dark time in my life and I was struggling with what to do next.

One of my clients had a property letting business, so I contacted her. I had £900 to my name and I was hoping that this would be enough for the deposit and first month's rent. Luckily for me it was and within a week, I had moved into my new house. All my friends and even my clients had heard what had happened and kindly donated items. Everything from a television to a washing machine, my house was liveable. I didn't have a bed to sleep in or a plate to eat off but, in time I had all the things that I needed and I could start to call this place home. After ten years living with someone, I'll be honest this took some adjusting to and I remember feeling very alone and very scared.

Ryan had just been released from jail and he came to live with me. He had always had a drug addiction from being about sixteen and had been in and out of prison all his life, but he was my brother. Sadly, after a month of been released he was back on the drugs and things escalated well beyond my wildest nightmares. Within just a few months he had committed over thirty-six burglaries in the local area of which I lived. I hung my head in shame, I couldn't believe what had become. Months passed and I'd not heard from Ryan even though I knew he was still in the area and still committing crimes. Then, I received a phone call from the police to say that he had been admitted to hospital and that he was under arrest. I called the hospital but they would not give me any information, not even what ward he was on. More months passed and I still knew nothing. That was until I received a phone call from Ryan himself. He was in prison; he was full of apologies as always, promised to change his ways but, to be honest the drugs had got the better of him like they had years ago. It was such a shame because to me he was still my little brother and if only people knew the real him.

Life was busy but life was now feeling good. I had broken away from a toxic marriage, had a business that was growing and I was starting to enjoy life again. I decided to treat myself and I went to a Happy Mondays gig in the local town. Foolishly I had been out all day drinking and looking back I should have gone home hours prior to the gig. But the gig was amazing. I was close up to the stage and I remember dancing and when my ankle gave way I fell to the floor. Slightly embarrassed I got up but I soon realised something was wrong. I had heard and felt the bone break. The door staff of the club automatically assumed I was drunk and asked me to leave but I kept trying to tell them I couldn't stand up. Luckily, they soon realised that I had injured myself due to the swelling of my ankle. They carried me outside and sat me on a chair. An ambulance was called and I was taken to hospital. I remained there for a few days, I had to have an operation to rectify the broken bone, it was 20th December 2018. I remember waking up after the operation and Fairy Tale of New York was playing on a nearby radio. Still under the influence of the anaesthetic I started to cry. Confused I asked the nurse where my husband and kids were? Then it hit me, it felt as if my world had come crashing down, I remembered I had left that life a few weeks prior.

My good friend Kirsty let me stay with her and looked after me. I was unable to weight bare for nine weeks. I had to close the office for a few weeks over the Christmas and New Year period as I was in no fit state to work. Life was challenging again. I had a broken ankle, filed for divorce, had a brother who was in prison for being a drug addict and committing crimes and I didn't realise at the time but I was very vulnerable.

I soon became involved with a man who turned out to be a very jealous, controlling, violent man. I had begun this relationship, as I believe, on the rebound from my separation and really, I ignored the warning signs. Just after a few weeks he became very controlling and jealous. On nights out he would start saying nasty comments towards me. If I went out with a friend, I was unsure how but he would post nasty comments on my social media. I soon realised he must have access to my passwords to be able to log on my social media account.

I tried to make this relationship work and booked a holiday for us in the March. We were due to go when I realised again that he was accessing my messages. I was in two minds whether to go but it had cost me a lot of money that I couldn't get back so I decided to put the worries I had to the back of my mind and go. It was the 23rd March 2019, what would have been my Dad's 60th Birthday. I have always raised a glass of whiskey to my Dad each year since he passed, and this day was no different. I was sitting in the sun relaxing by the pool when a bird flew over and sat on my table. It's worth pointing out I have a phobia of birds and this made me jump back out of my seat. I seem to remember swearing at this poor bird. This what I thought was a little comical incident didn't go down well with my partner. He started to scream and shout at me, telling me I'm supposed to be a lady and should not swear. He followed by saying my council estate upbringing would ruin my business! I was already struggling with today, my Dad's Birthday, now I was hurt and embarrassed at being shouted at in public, so I quietly got up and walked away. I spent the rest of the day on my own sunbathing. I ate lunch alone and later that afternoon I called my daughter, I also spoke to my estranged husband. He knew what day it was and offered comfort to me. We both said that we loved each other and would talk when I was back to England. That moment I knew that I wanted to try and make my marriage work. That evening the man I was on holiday with became aggressive and violent. He knocked a cigarette out of my hand and tried to burn me with it. I asked him to leave me alone but it escalated out of control. He tried hitting me then threw a plate at me. Fearing for my safety and my life I knew I had to leave. I went to get my passport but it had gone, so had my money. He had hidden it all. I left the apartment and went to reception and asked for another room. They had no rooms available. I didn't know what to do. I called both my brother and Kirsty who were both concerned for my safety. I tried to book a flight home but there were no flights available. We were due to fly home the next evening so I had no choice but to go back to the apartment. I got on the sofa and stayed there the whole night. The following morning, he was full of remorse. You know how it goes, promise never to do it again, I just wanted my passport back, which I got. I spent the rest of that day scared but very wary of him. I just wanted to go home, back to England.

I could not wait to board that plane and feel safe. The flight back was made in almost silence, I spoke only when I needed to. We arrived back in England and I was scared. All I wanted was for him to leave but I was weak, I was being controlled in a very clever way. I let him stay and that was the worst mistake I could have made. It wasn't long before the mental abuse started all over again. Deep down I didn't want him. I yearned for my husband and my marriage, but I was too scared and weak to ask him to leave. I very often ask myself how can someone control you to the point you can no longer think for yourself? My friends around me could see what was going on but, for some reason, I tried to convince myself it would all turn out right!

I was due to go out with Kirsty for a girl's night out. But he had other ideas. It all started again. I'd had enough and I found the courage to tell him to leave. He wouldn't go. I threatened him with the police. "I will go and leave you alone if you let me in your bed" he yelled. I felt trapped and again like years before I found myself in a situation where a man had forced himself on me and there was nothing I could do. The next morning, he left with all his belongings and I dared to sigh and think to myself it was all over, he'd gone and that was the end, but no it wasn't. Later that day I started to receive threating phone calls and text messages. I ignored them at first but then they became more serious and I had no alternative but to contact the police. I was being threatened with revenge porn. I was on the verge of a breakdown and in such a dark place.

Kirsty came round after a call from my brother and she found me on the bedroom floor, crying hysterically. She sat with me for hours whilst I cried and poured out all the upset and fear. I had hit rock bottom, I felt there was no way out. It took me a very long time to get out of this dark place, but from somewhere deep down in me I found the strength.

"New beginnings for this boss"

May 2019, I was still feeling lost and had a few dark days, but I was determined to get back into work and continue to build an empire. Work was growing and I was busy so, I decided to take someone on as work experience with the view of a job if they were suitable. Interviews arranged and the day arrived. This girl walked into my office, she was that nervous she was shaking and tears filled her eyes. I saw myself in her as a young sixteen-year-old, I connected with her straight away. I knew I wanted to give her a chance, and I am so glad I did, it was the best decision I had made in a long time. I have always been a big believer in giving back and what you put out into the universe you will get back tenfold.

Now I am not saying this year was easy, Ryan was back in prison, sentenced to ten years this time. I was going through a divorce. As hard as I'd tried, I hadn't been able to save my marriage. I found out my husband had committed the most awful betrayal and he was now living with my ex-neighbour who previously I had classed as a particularly good friend. I'd lost contact with my children except one daughter, Rhianna, who came to live with me. And it didn't stop there. I was still experiencing problems with my ex-partner, he continued to threatened me with revenge porn; apparently when we were together, he had taken photos of me when I was asleep, he tried blackmailing me to sleep with him or he would post them on to my business page. He damaged my home, his idea of revenge was to kick my doors and windows in. I felt like I was drowning, friends didn't know me, I dyed my hair, got a nose piercing, and possibly drank too much. Basically I was spiralling out of control.

One day I was scrolling through social media, nursing a hell of a hangover when I came across a quote, which read… "travel alone just once, it will be the most exhilarating yet scary thing you will ever do", and in that moment, I said myself, "if I don't get a grip and do something now, I'll lose it all". No time to waste I went online booked a holiday and my flight was in six hours' time! I quickly packed, got in my car and drove to the airport. I didn't tell anyone except Rhianna. I was so nervous yet excited. I updated my social media after I had landed and was settled at my hotel. My phone went crazy. I had to face time friends because they did not believe I was sitting in Gran Canaria. The sun was just what I needed. I had been to see a lady for some holistic treatment a few days prior and she said that she could feel the hurt in my stomach and the sun would heal me. She was right I had four days to myself and it was the best thing I ever did; I honestly believe it saved my life. I sat on the beach for hours watching the tide go back and forth. I openly cried and let all the hurt and anger out and I felt like a weight had been lifted. I sat in the sun and for the first time in a long time, I felt calm, relaxed and at peace.

After a leisurely stroll I bought a small ball, a paper pad and a writing pen from the local shop. That night I sat and wrote a letter to my husband. I told him I forgave him and that I had to let him go to move on and make a new life. I tied the letter around the ball and secured it with a hair band. That night I set my alarm and at 6am I was on the beach. The beach was empty and so peaceful, just a few locals taking their morning jog. I picked a song on my phone that meant a lot to me, Ordinary People by Bugzy Malone, I pressed play and I let the music play for a few minutes then I spoke. I let out into the universe it was time for me to let go and I threw the ball into the sea. I was told sometime in my life that if you worship the goddess of the sea by throwing her something, in turn she will throw you something back. I believed at that moment I was healed. I spent the last day on the beach in my safe place watching the waves crashing back and forth, the sun shining so bright and the heat touched my face. I felt amazing. I flew back home with a fresh attitude and with a new sense of life. I knew I was stronger and ready to face anything. My thoughts were positive and again as when my dad passed, I decided to channel my hurt into a positive.

I got my head back into work as this was my haven, my safe place. June 2019 came and the office was inundated with new clients. The word had spread and I had taken on clients from Nottingham, Ireland, and Scotland. I then had a meeting with another lady in Manchester through my client over there, and you know when you just meet someone, and you know good things are going to come from this. My phone never stopped with new clients I was commuting from Chesterfield to Manchester every other day to sign up clients. It was then I decided it was about time I opened an office in Manchester.

1st July 2019 the Hayes Worth and Stone Manchester was born. I had made enough money at the main office to be able to invest in a Manchester base. I had employed staff in both offices and I commuted and worked between the two. I was gaining new clients by the day. My social media was constantly advertising my business and booking in meetings. My client base had tripled in a few months and I had even taken on clients in Spain and Australia. With a fresh mind set I felt that I could achieve anything that I put my mind to.

Not many people in my home town really knew about my Manchester office plus I wanted to create a buzz in Manchester itself. So, I explained to Kirsty what I had in mind and asked if she wanted to come with me to Manchester. She jumped at the offer. We had our makeup done professionally, I bought a new dress, red of course, we drove to Manchester that day but we didn't tell anyone. I treated us to a five-star meal complete with champagne in local restaurant just around the corner from the new office. We took a photo of us with the champagne and photos of the new office, then I announced it on my social media. The response was amazing, it felt so good. I had achieved what some had said was the unachievable, I had proven them all wrong.

"The girl had made it"

After possibly one of the worst years of my life, personally I am so glad I decided to keep working and channel the bad energy into good things. I wanted now to give back. I always told myself I would so, that year I sponsored local football teams, swimming clubs, helped the homeless and donated to many different events and charites. My goal as always been to never forget where I came from, never forget my roots. The experiences you gain growing up set you up later in life. These experiences mould you into the person you are today, for me I decided to turn all my childhood and adult [bad] experiences into a positive, and I vow to this day to help people when and where I can. Homelessness and addiction play heavy on my heart because of Ryan and Dad, and just by my chance one evening whilst I was on social media, I had a message. A friend of mine from Stockport had mentioned me to a guy that was wanting some help with his accounts and by chance, he was part of a recovery charity which he had just help set up. I was very interested and we had a "meeting" over the phone. We had an instant chemistry and I arranged a face-to-face meeting to hear more about the recovery outreach service. I headed over to Stockport the next day, I believe that in your life you will meet someone who in one way or another you will just connect with, and not in a sexual or romantic way but someone you can have a real understanding and connection on a level that when two worlds resonate and you are destined for big things. This is how I felt after our meeting in Stockport. I immediately donated three thousand pounds to the recovery outreach, Dry Wave Recovery. The main director who I had the meeting with has had his own struggles in the past. To this day we have remained very dear friends. My three thousand pounds helped to fund the Dry Digital Radio talk show they hold each week, as well as many other events. Sadly, due to the 2019 pandemic, events have had to be cancelled but this has given Dry Wave time to put together rescue packs for the recovery community.

I was asked to tell my story on the Dry Wave Recovery talk show. Now my story is not about recovery, I have never had an addiction problem, however Ryan and my Dad had so, my story was broadcasted out there hopefully to inspire the listeners to reach out and ask for our help. The show was a massive success, it was live on all social media platforms, I really enjoyed telling my story of struggle and going for your dreams.

Following the show more was to come. I was asked if I would become the financial director of Dry Wave. This was an honour; I am fully behind the initiative Dry Wave stands for and love to help people. I was also asked to appear in a music video funded by Dry Wave, it was my friend the main director who wrote the song, local patrons of Dry Wave were also invited to appear. The filming went great, we had a fantastic day connecting with men and women in recovery and hearing their stories. Watching someone you love destroy themselves with drugs is not pleasant to witness so their stories gave me hope that one day Ryan would be clean and drug free. I appeared on the talk show again later in the year. Now, because of this radio experience, it gave me a newfound love for radio and broadcasting.

Later in the year I was approached by a new local radio station in Chesterfield. At first, I was hesitant, and was not too sure if I could commit the task. However, I decided to give the radio broadcasting a go, it was a great success. I was offered a Thursday night show and soon after I was offered a prime-time Saturday afternoon show, not bad for a girl who had a terrible stammer as a child. I was now broadcasting to thousands of people twice a week. I did not stop there. One of my clients owns a multi-six figure beauty business as well as an international coach to thousands of women. I was asked to appear with her in a podcast show. This podcast was to break the stigma of accountants and to inspire businesswomen with my story, it was a fantastic opportunity to offer my accountancy services and make it accessible to all sizes of businesses, the podcast was a massive success. I gained so many new clients. The reviews from the podcast were outstanding. It's a real comfort to me that I can have my career, inspire women to follow my lead and at the same time just be myself.

Another achievement for myself and my business, I would say the biggest in my eyes, was when I was able to sponsor a Stoke City player, seven years to the day when I promised my Dad, he would see his name at Stoke City Football Club. I had my picture with the player I had sponsored, my business name was in the program as well as all around the stadium. I even got to meet all the team and have photos taken. It was a bitter sweet day but I was immensely proud of what I had achieved. I had a tour of the ground and I took a piece of my Dad's hair that I'd taken from him when he passed, I knelt on the side of the pitch and pushed his hair gently into the soil of the pitch with a soft whisper "back were you belong dad". Everything I have ever tried to achieve in my business has been driven in honouring my late Dad and hopefully if he's watching, making him proud of me.

Two months later following many late nights and extremely hard work I'd now signed up my 700th client, not bad from a girl from a council estate! One of my dreams was to go to New York City, and Christmas Eve 2019 I achieved that dream. I always thought years ago that a girl like me would never see the world especially New York but, here I was, tickets booked. I took Rhianna with me to "The Big Apple" for Christmas. Excitement flushed the both of us as we sat in a five star hotel with a glass of champagne waiting to head over to Heathrow airport and fly off to America. The night before Rhianna and I flew, we travelled to London and had a day shopping. We walked through the streets of London when I turned and saw Harrods, "shall we go in?" I said, before long there we were walking through the departments of Harrods. As a treat I bought both Rhianna and myself a purse each. I had always wanted to go into Harrods but never thought in my lifetime I would be able to afford to purchase an item. Christmas in London is amazing. Rhianna had never been to the "Big Smoke" so we made the best of our time there, we walked over past Big Ben and the London eye then a walk around Soho and Piccadilly Circus, that's when the saying I'd heard on so many occasions clicked, "it's like Piccadilly Circus in here". The crowds were immense, almost too busy. Rhianna loved London. We finished off in China Town for tea. Christmas Eve morning soon came around and we headed to start our dream Christmas break in the "Big Apple". I blame watching Home Alone as kid, that started my dream of the Big Apple. The feeling you get when you step off the plane. It's cold, fresh and just feels very much like Christmas. Our hotel was in the centre of Times Square and the views were phenomenal. We woke up on Christmas Day morning, I had to pinch myself. I remember thinking to myself, dreams can come true. I had always dreamed of waking up in New York City on Christmas Day ever since I was a six-year-old girl after watching Home Alone Lost in New York. I rose and went to get a coffee and bagel from the hotel restaurant, then I walked around Times Square. It was 6 am in the morning and I just stood still for a second and a tear rolled down my cheek. The feeling I had overwhelmed me. I remember thinking to myself, a girl like me from my background not only is it Christmas day but it's Christmas day here in New York. It was one of the best days of my life and I felt immensely proud of what I had achieved.

Still, I could not resist doing a little marketing for my business. Before going out to New York I'd had a tee-shirt printed with my logo on and I walked around Central Park Christmas day morning wearing it! Christmas Day dinner was at a small American dinner, quarter pounder with fries and a milkshake! After dinner we headed to the Empire State Building and spent a few hours taking in all the breath-taking views. Life could not get any better than this, dreams do come true. Christmas Day night we headed down to Brooklyn. We walked over the Brooklyn Bridge back in to Manhattan, then made our way up Seventh Avenue to the Rocka Fella tree. The streets of New York were full of people and musicians playing Christmas music, the atmosphere was magical, really indescribable.

Boxing Day was magical but also surreal, we headed down to Ground Zero, Wall Street, and even decide to take the train to New Jersey for a few hours. We finished Boxing Day off with a shopping trip to one of the most famous department stores in the world. Our feet were sore and we were so tired from all the walking, but we did not care we carried on, after all we were "in the city that never sleeps". We had stumbled upon a small Christmas market in Bryant Park, and this is where I purchased a notebook. A beautiful buck bound book with a picture of the Empire State Building on the front. Inside just blank pages, it was perfect. I would use this to write down all my goals for 2020. That evening back in the hotel I sat on the bed and began to write. I wanted to be debt free in 2020, I wanted to sign up a thousand clients by 2021. On a personal level I wanted to heal from the past few years and learn to love again, and so on. By May 2020, I had achieved all the goals except the client sign up but this was ok, I knew I had time and that I would hit that goal with hard work and determination.

After a fantastic break and with the January [accountancy] deadline looming, I decided to go in to 2020 with a focused and determined attitude. The only way I knew how to action this was to focus on the final accolade to my Dad. After a few weeks of planning and number crunching I was in a financial position to set up my third office. I did it, I opened office number three in Stoke on Trent 20th January 2020. I often wish Dad was around to see the Stoke office but I know deep down he is watching, probably from the football ground! All this hard work had really begun to show me results, I had my third site in my ever-growing empire. I have never been shy of hard work and this new site gave me even more drive and determination than ever. I did not stop there. I decided that the sky was the limit literally. My next step may shock you, it did a lot of people but I took the steps to become a trainee pilot! From my childhood and all the weekends spent with Dad and Ryan at the aviation viewing park at Manchester Airport, this had always been one of my dreams, to be a licensed pilot and fly a plane. I met my pilot instructor; my first was a classroom lesson, we covered all the safety procedures and the etiquette whilst you are airborne. There was so much to take in and I started to feel very overwhelmed. We headed out on the airfield, to my plane, things were about to get very real. Before anything all the flight's safety checks must be completed and this flight was no different. The instructor showed me how to check the plane over and what must be reported and recorded before each flight. I got into the aircraft and sat in the left-hand side, planes have two controls, my head set was steady for me to radio through to air traffic control and the final safety checks were made, it was time for take-off.

We made our way down the runway, turned around at the end and we were ready to taxi along before take-off. I remember thinking to myself as we took off, this is really happening. I had a feeling of shear excitement but yes nervous at the same time. I was completely overwhelmed. The evening sky was perfect, the sun was starting to set and not a cloud in the sky. The instructor asked me if I would like to take control of the plane. I was flying my first plane over Sheffield and Chesterfield. I was asked by my instructor to make a left and then a right turn in the sky. This was one of the most amazing experiences I have had. At one point I became completely overwhelmed, and I had to ask my instructor to take back control of the aircraft and I began to cry, not through fear but a sheer feeling of adrenaline and that over whelming sense of achievement. My first flight had come to an end. I was excited to hear how my instructor rated my first flight. He told me I was a perfect candidate to be put forward for my pilot licence, I was overjoyed and excited. I booked my next lesson and purchased all the books required for the exams.

I thought 2020 was going to be the year I would pass my pilot licence but, unfortunately, none of us could have prepared ourselves for the up-and-coming months that followed.

The comeback is greater than the set back.

The year 2020 saw what we all soon knew as the new normal. A global pandemic had forced many businesses to close for months. Luckily for me my business could be run from anywhere as long as I have a laptop and internet. The global pandemic was an unprecedented time and many of my clients were in financial disarray. Rather than taking a back seat, I made a promise to myself that I would help as many people as I could during the COVID-19 pandemic. I began to post updates as soon as they came in from the government and put together free information packs for all my clients. The workload was immense and after working eighteen-hour days for three months the cracks finally started to show.

April is one of my busiest times usually, but on top of the usual workload, I was the person so many clients relied on for the daily information on my social media from financial help available to updates from the government. Near the end of May, my body had finally had enough. I was not sleeping, I was over worked and stressed. I needed to take time out for myself. It was only because of my friend Kirsty that I stopped. A mini-intervention was made and I took some much-needed time to regroup and sleep. I was exhausted and really not taking particularly good care of myself and it showed. After some much needed respite I was back at work. Another few months had passed and the workload had still not eased. Most of the businesses around were still unable to open and my own business started to be affected financially. I knew I had to carry on providing the same level of great service to my clients and I had to trust the universe that things would be ok. The UK slowly started to re-open and businesses could start to trade again. My own financial burden was lifted. It was time to get back to what I did best. With all the free advice I gave out during the first lockdown and my constant update to everyone, my name and my business was out there. Hayes Worth and

Stone was a name people now knew, things seemed to be great but as always life sometimes throws you a spanner and turns your world upside down.

September and during the global pandemic I were so secure in my business that I opened my fourth site to HWS empire, this time in London. The London office opened and was making a profit as were my other three offices. I was commuting between Clay Cross, Manchester, Stoke on Trent and London. Life was good.

I was single after ten years of marriage, so I decided to live a little. I decided to sign up to a dating site. Much to my surprise I began talking to a guy in London. During one of my journeys to the London office we met up for a drink. I ended up staying over, not my usual style but I was happy and went with the flow. We had exchanged numbers but to be honest I was not looking for any kind of relationship. I left the next morning, homeward bound back up north to crack on with my day. Things soon fizzled out with me and my London guy, which was fine on my part, I had an empire to run.

Four weeks later I made a shocking discovery I was pregnant. I immediately went to Kirsty's house to tell her my news, she was elated, she started to cry which then set me off crying. This was the last thing I thought I wanted but after the initial shock I was over the moon. I was going to be a mother and experience childbirth. Not ideal at my age I know, but I knew I was financially secure, had an amazing support bubble with Rhianna and Kirsty. With my telephone appointment with the midwife, everything was going well. Like most, I had terrible morning sickness, but I dealt with that. My nickname for my bump was, Baby London. I was overjoyed but at the same time I found it so hard to tell anyone. Being super excited, I booked in for a six-week scan in Sheffield, Kirsty came with me. I had never had a scan before this was such a special moment and I shared it with my best friend Kirsty. We saw the baby's heartbeat, both of us cried. Then I was given my due date............. 23rd March, Dad's birthday, I was so overjoyed.

A couple of weeks later I felt unwell. I had some pains in my lower stomach. Worriedly I called 111. I was told to go up to the hospital the next day for a routine scan. The following morning before I made the journey to the hospital, I popped to the local shop, in there I saw a rainbow candle holder, not sure why, my hormones must have been all over the place because as soon as I saw it, I cried. I had to buy the candle, I don't know why I just did. I just thought to myself this must be a sign that all is going to be alright. I got to the hospital and I had my scan. The next words spoken by the nurse will never ever leave me as long as I live. She looked towards me and said she needed to get a second opinion. My heart sank, I knew then what was happening. The door opened and a second nurse came into the room. She confirmed my worst nightmare, my baby had no heartbeat. My whole world came crashing down in a split second. I had not felt like this since losing Dad back in 2014.

I was taken to a small room and the nurses explained to me that I'd had a miscarriage. The shock overwhelmed me so much I couldn't speak. Due to the COVID-19 pandemic I was all alone at the hospital, I had no one to hold me or comfort me. I was sitting in a daze in my car but for the life of me I couldn't remember how I got there. I called Kirsty then Ryan. Where I got the strength from to tell them the devastating news I had just received, I will never know. Ryan isn't a man of many words, he asked if I was ok and that was it. Kirsty, well that was different. We are so connected that if I am hurting she is too, she was as devastated as I was. How I'll never know, I made my way home. The time was here, five days after my scan I was back at the hospital for an operation to remove my baby. I was anxious and could not believe what was going to happen today. I should have been nine weeks pregnant and full of excitement for another new chapter in my life, but instead the universe had other plans for me. I knew I had to be strong and put on my suit of armour, I had to get through this. Later that day I was back home and Kirsty brought her son, my godson, to see me. I now needed to take a few weeks away from work. Slowly, each day I became stronger and tried to get back to normal. My drive was, my baby would not be forgotten. I arranged a service, in a way this was my closure but, I would always have a place I could go. The service was beautiful, I had eight rainbow balloons released at the end of the service.

Again, I found myself in grief and the only way I knew how to cope with a loss was to work. This had always been my solution in the past and I knew that this would work for me. I went back to work after a few weeks off and focused on continuing to build my empire along with giving as much as I could to the local community.

I found a new focus; the news was full of providing meals for children. I did more and donated to the Feed Britain Campaign as well local charities helping families in crisis. This pandemic had put not only us, the UK, in crisis but the whole world was suffering the same. Giving back helps me feel a better person. I empathise with another person's personal situation as I have found myself in many difficult situations over the years. It's my way of answering someone else prayers, although in all honesty at that time I was in need of my prayers been answered. I continued to gather strength and carry on with my charity work donating further to more homeless charities. I had an idea, with Kirsty together we completed a charity walk for shelter and made a fair donation for the local food banks.

Lockdown three was now upon us and again, as in previous lockdowns, I supported the local community by giving free advice and all the assistance I could regarding the local grants available. Work for me never stopped during the pandemic. I have been lucky enough to have a successful business during a global pandemic. With all the uncertainty in the world, if you can be anything, be kind.

It is now the 23rd January 2021 and with all honesty I can say my journey is far from over. Throughout my life I have fallen in love and lost love. I have lost people dear to me, some may have been a blessing but some not. I have been lied to and used in the most horrific ways but, in the end if you keep a positive attitude and be determined, work hard and never let anyone tell you that you cannot do anything, you really can achieve anything you want too. I am living proof of that. Stay humble and never ever forget your roots. Always give back when you can and I truly believe the universe will give you what is destined to be yours in time.

I am looking forward to the future and one day an office in New York. As I sit at this very moment in my beautiful new home, listening to my podcast with a coffee, I think to myself AKA. WHAT A LIFE.

Bullet beans to big dreams never forget that.
Gem xxx

Printed in Great Britain
by Amazon